ASSERTIVE DISCIPLINE®

When Lee Canter and Marlene Canter first developed Assertive Discipline in 1976, their goal was to help teachers manage disruptive behavior in a firm and positive manner. Over the years, the principles of the program have been expanded and adjusted to meet the changing needs of teachers and their students. Today, the Assertive Discipline program goes beyond managing disruptive behavior. It teaches you how to prevent behavior problems from occurring and how to provide the positive support students need for making responsible decisions regarding their behavior. When we enable students to be successful in school, we are empowering them with skills that will become the foundation for their self-esteem and future success.

Teacher's Plan Book Plus #1

The key to successful behavior management is planning. This *Teacher's Plan Book Plus #1* is an all-new and revised version of our original *Teacher's Plan Book Plus #1* which has been used by over 500,000 teachers. This book will help you to integrate your planning of positive behavior management strategies with your regular weekly planning. By mapping out the steps you will take each week to ensure a well-managed classroom, you will increase your effectiveness in the classroom as well as the success of your students.

The first part of this book is a simple, step-by-step guide to creating a classroom discipline plan which will serve as a foundation for all your behavior management efforts.

Next you'll find traditional weekly planning pages—*with lots of pluses!* Each week you'll find an Assertive Discipline implementation tip, a motivating positive reinforcement idea, space for jotting daily reminders, and room to record specific discipline notes.

Following the weekly planning pages are additional positive recognition ideas, strategies for dealing with chronic behavior problems, and convenient record sheets. (Review these materials before the school year starts so you will know where they are when you need them.)

Table of Contents

Y0-BEM-783

Seven Steps to a Successful Start of School

1 CREATE A CLASSROOM DISCIPLINE PLAN

2 PRESENT YOUR PLAN TO YOUR ADMINISTRATOR

3 TEACH YOUR DISCIPLINE PLAN TO YOUR STUDENTS

4 COMMUNICATE YOUR DISCIPLINE PLAN TO PARENTS

5 PREPARE A DISCIPLINE PLAN FOR SUBSTITUTES

6 IMPLEMENT YOUR CLASSROOM DISCIPLINE PLAN

7 REVIEW ASSERTIVE DISCIPLINE GUIDELINES

START SMART

1 CREATE A CLASSROOM DISCIPLINE PLAN

The first step to a great start of school is to create a classroom discipline plan. A classroom discipline plan is a system that allows you to spell out the behaviors you expect from students and what they can expect from you in return. Such a plan provides a framework around which all of your behavior management efforts can be organized.

Establish Rules for Your Classroom

Your first task in creating a classroom discipline plan is to determine the general rules for your classroom. General classroom rules are those rules that are in place all day long—throughout all activities. General classroom rules are important because they let your students know exactly what your behavior expectations are and put the responsibility for choosing appropriate behavior in their hands.

Before the year begins, take time to identify the behaviors you expect of all students at all times. Follow the guidelines below.

Choose rules that are observable.

Address behaviors that you can clearly see. Vaguely stated expectations may mean one thing to one student, and an entirely different thing to another. Vague rules can often cause more problems and open the door for arguments.

For example:

Observable Rules
- Keep hands and feet to yourself.
- Be in your seat when the bell rings.
- No yelling or screaming.

Vague Expectations
- Be kind to other students.
- No fooling around when class starts.
- No unnecessary talking.

Choose rules that apply throughout the day.

General classroom rules are rules that apply all day, no matter what activity is taking place. These are rules that students are expected to follow at all times.

Include the rule "Follow directions" in your general classroom rules.

This rule will help ensure that students follow any direction you might give throughout the day (see guidelines on page 7 for determining specific directions for your classroom).

Here are some appropriate general classroom rules for different grade levels:

Grades K–3
- Follow directions.
- Keep hands, feet and objects to yourself.
- Do not leave the room without permission.
- No swearing or teasing.
- No yelling or screaming.

Grades 4–6
- Follow directions.
- Keep hands, feet and objects to yourself.
- No swearing or teasing.
- Be in your seat when the bell rings.
- Bring all necessary materials to class.

Grades 7-12
- Follow directions.
- No swearing or teasing.
- Be in your seat when the bell rings.

Now list the general rules for your classroom.

(Keep to a maximum of five.)

_____

_____

_____

_____

Determine Positive Reinforcement for Your Classroom

Once you've determined your classroom rules and specific directions, your next step is to determine how you will positively recognize students for following them. Positive recognition is the sincere and meaningful attention you give a student for behaving according to your expectations.

Consistently used, positive recognition will:

- Encourage students to behave appropriately.
- Increase students' self-esteem.
- Reduce behavior problems.
- Create a positive classroom climate.
- Help you teach appropriate behavior.
- Help you establish positive relationships with your students.

Five ways to positively recognize students:

Praise

Praise should be your #1 choice in positive recognition. When you take the time to say something positive to a student, you convey the message, "I care about you, I notice your good efforts, and I'm proud of you."

"Nicki, you lined up quickly and quietly. That really helps us go to lunch on time. Thanks for being so cooperative."

Positive Notes and Phone Calls

Letting students know that you will send positive notes and make positive phone calls to their parents is a great motivator for good behavior. Communicating with parents about their child's good efforts at school helps establish a positive rapport with parents and increases your chances of gaining their support should a problem arise.

Special Privileges

Recognize good behavior by rewarding students with activities they particularly enjoy. Ask students what privileges they would like to earn.

Here are some examples:

- Free time
- Extra computer time
- Correcting papers
- Special art activity
- First in line
- Caretaker of the class pet
- Teacher's assistant
- Class monitor
- Cross-grade tutor
- Read to kindergarten class
- Share something brought in from home

Behavior Awards

Present awards that recognize students for their good behavior. The award can be designed to recognize appropriate behavior in general or a specific behavior such as, following directions, listening attentively, cooperating in a small group activity or being seated when the bell rings.

Tangible Rewards

Use of tangible rewards such as stickers, prizes and treats is not recommended on a consistent basis. However, tangible rewards are particularly effective when students are overly excited or when a student is not responding to other forms of positive recognition. Use tangible rewards with discretion and always pair them with your sincere words of praise.

Guidelines for determining your positives:

1. Select positives with which you are most comfortable (for example, praising a student for appropriate behavior instead of giving him or her candy).

2. The recognition should be meaningful to the student—something he or she appreciates and enjoys.

3. The recognition should be provided as soon as possible after the student exhibits the appropriate behavior. (You can delay rewards with older students.)

4. Positives should be provided as consistently as possible.

5. Plan ahead of time which specific appropriate behaviors merit reinforcement. Remember to positively recognize students' efforts as well as their achievements.

See pages 94-96 for more positive recognition ideas.

List the positives you will use.

_____

_____

_____

_____

_____

Determine Disciplinary Consequences for Your Classroom

By carefully planning consequences, you will know in advance what you will do when students misbehave, and you won't be caught off guard or left wondering how to respond to problem behavior. Also, students will know exactly what to expect when they choose not to follow the rules.

Guidelines for choosing consequences for your classroom:

- Consequences must be something that students do not like, but must never be physically or psychologically harmful.

- Consequences must be presented to students as a choice. When a teacher gives students a choice, the responsibility is placed where it belongs, with the student.

- Consequences do not have to be severe to be effective. It is the inevitability of the consequence, not the severity, that makes it effective. Minimal consequences are most effective and easiest to implement.

- Consequences should be organized into a discipline hierarchy as part of your classroom discipline plan. A discipline hierarchy lists consequences in the order in which they will be imposed for disruptive behavior within a day. This hierarchy is progressive, starting with a warning. The consequences then gradually become more substantial for the second, third, fourth and fifth times that a student chooses to disrupt.

The hierarchy should include calling parents and sending the student to the principal, if appropriate. It should also include a severe clause to be used if a student fights or refuses to do what he or she is told. The severe clause may be, for example, sending the student immediately to the principal.

Sample discipline hierarchies:

The following hierarchies list consequences to be imposed the first, second, third, fourth and fifth times a student disrupts or is continually off task during the course of the school day:

Grades K-3

First time:	Warning
Second time:	5 minutes working away from the group
Third time:	10 minutes working away from the group
Fourth time:	Call parents
Fifth time:	Send to principal
Severe clause:	Send to principal

Grades 4-6

First time:	Warning
Second time:	10 minutes working away from the group
Third time:	15 minutes working away from the group, write in behavior journal
Fourth time:	Call parents
Fifth time:	Send to principal
Severe clause:	Send to principal

Grades 7-12

First time:	Warning
Second time:	Stay in class 1 minute after the bell
Third time:	Stay in class 2 minutes after the bell, write in behavior journal
Fourth time:	Call parents
Fifth time:	Send to principal
Severe clause:	Send to principal

Now list the consequences you will use.

First time: _____

Second time: _____

Third time: _____

Fourth time: _____

Fifth time: _____

Severe clause: _____

_____

2 PRESENT YOUR PLAN TO YOUR ADMINISTRATOR

A key to effective discipline is knowing that you will have the support of your administrator. Prepare a copy of your classroom discipline plan for your administrator's approval. Make sure that you and your administrator are clear as to the role he or she will play in your plan. Discuss your expectations of what will take place when you send a student to the principal. Ask for his or her input and be open to any suggested changes. Also, discuss what will happen if the principal is not in the building.

3 TEACH YOUR DISCIPLINE PLAN TO YOUR STUDENTS

By creating your classroom discipline plan, you have clarified for yourself the appropriate behaviors you expect of students, how you will recognize appropriate behavior, and how you will deal with students' misbehavior. In order for students to be successful in choosing responsible behavior, they too must have a clear understanding of what you expect from them and of what they can expect from you in return.

Plan a lesson for teaching your classroom discipline plan to your students on the first day of school.

In order for students to clearly understand your plan and how it works, and to be successful in meeting your expectations, you must take the time to teach your plan to them just as you would teach any other subject or skill.

Use the following steps to develop your lesson:

Make a classroom discipline plan poster for your classroom.

Write your rules, positives and consequences on a large poster such as the one shown below. Use the poster as a visual aid as you proceed through your lesson. After the lesson, display the poster in a prominent location in your classroom to serve as a constant reminder to students. When visitors are in your classroom, they, too, will be aware of your classroom rules.

Note: For very young children, place pictures next to each rule.

CLASSROOM RULES
1 _____
2 _____
3 _____
4 _____
5 _____

POSITIVES
1 _____
2 _____
3 _____
4 _____
5 _____

CONSEQUENCES
1 _____
2 _____
3 _____
4 _____
5 _____
6 _____

LEE CANTER'S ASSERTIVE DISCIPLINE ®

Draw students' attention to your classroom discipline plan poster.

Tell students that the poster shows a plan you have created to help them behave appropriately in your classroom. Explain that this plan will be in effect at all times and must be followed every day, all year long.

Explain why you need rules.

Tell students that the first part of the plan deals with rules for your classroom. Discuss rules students are already familiar with—at home, in the community (laws)—and why they are so important. Talk about the need for classroom rules—to provide a safe and orderly environment where you can teach and students can learn.

Explain your classroom rules.

Clearly explain each rule listed on the poster and why it is important. Discuss and demonstrate (for younger students) what the appropriate behavior "looks like," "sounds like" and "feels like."

Check for understanding.

Have students explain and demonstrate each rule. Praise them for correct responses.

Explain how you will positively recognize students for following rules and directions.

Tell students that you know they can be successful at following the rules and that it will be your pleasure to recognize and reward them for choosing appropriate behavior in the classroom. Enthusiastically explain each positive listed in your plan.

Explain why you have consequences.

In a firm and caring manner, let students know that you are serious about your expectations in the classroom. Tell them that consequences are an important part of the plan because they help students to be more successful in choosing appropriate behavior. Emphasize that consequences will be issued to students only as a result of their own choices.

Explain the consequences and how they will be implemented.

Explain exactly what will occur the first, second, third, fourth and fifth times a student disrupts. Explain your severe clause. Point out to students that consequences are not carried over from day to day. Students return to school each day with a clean slate—an opportunity to choose appropriate behavior and enjoy the rewards of their good choices.

Check for understanding.

Ask students to describe each consequence and explain how consequences will be imposed. Ask students if they have any questions.

Express your confidence in students' ability to make appropriate choices.

The manner in which you present your discipline plan to your students will set the tone for your classroom. Be positive! Let students know you believe they will make the right choices and help to make this a terrific year for your class.

4 COMMUNICATE YOUR DISCIPLINE PLAN TO PARENTS

Parents are the most important people in their child's life. Their support is critical to their child's academic and behavioral success. If parents are to become partners in their children's education, they must be well-informed about your classroom discipline plan and about their child's experiences at school.

Use the following strategies to communicate your classroom discipline plan to parents and establish ongoing communication between home and school.

Send a copy of your classroom discipline plan to parents.

The first day of school send home a letter to introduce yourself to parents, expressing your commitment to their child and sharing enthusiasm for the year ahead. Outline your plan and provide a detachable sign-off portion for parents to verify that they've read and understand your plan.

Share good news with parents.

Parents often receive news from school only when there is a problem. Send home positive notes and make positive phone calls early in the school year to let parents know their child is off to a good start. Continue your positive communication with parents all year long. Use the Positive Parent Communication Log on page 102 to keep track of the contact you've made.

QUICK NOTE to Parents

To: Mr. & Mrs. Tagert,
Just a quick note to tell you how pleased I am that John has turned in all of his homework this week. Great job!
Mrs. Janata
Signed

Contact parents at the first sign of a problem.

Send a letter, place a phone call, or set up a conference the moment a problem arises. Do not wait until parent-teacher conferences or report card time. The problem will only get worse. If you're not sure if you should contact the parent, use the "your own child" test. Simply ask yourself, "Would I want to be contacted if this were my child?"

Work with parents to solve behavior problems.

When a problem arises, meet with parents to develop a plan of action for solving the problem. Plan what you will say to the parent. Follow the guidelines on page 79.

Show your appreciation for parental support.

Parents need positive reinforcement too. Send home a note or make a quick call thanking parents who have been supportive of your behavior management efforts.

5 PREPARE A DISCIPLINE PLAN FOR SUBSTITUTES

To ensure consistency in your classroom management, even when you are not present, prepare a classroom discipline plan for substitutes. Make sure that a copy is left with the office. Put another copy in this Plan Book or tape it to the top of your desk.

6 IMPLEMENT YOUR CLASSROOM DISCIPLINE PLAN

You've created your classroom discipline plan and communicated it to your principal and to parents. You've taught your plan to your students and posted it in your classroom. You are now ready to put your plan into action each and every day of the school year. Use the following strategies to maximize your success in implementing your classroom discipline plan.

Determine Specific Directions for Your Classroom

You've listed the general rules for your classroom. These are the expectations that will be in effect all day long. The most important of these classroom rules is "Follow directions." As activities continually change throughout the day, so do your expectations. It is important to determine precisely what your expectations are for each routine procedure and classroom activity.

By determining clear and specific directions, students will know exactly how you expect them to behave at all times, and you will have better control over every situation.

Here are some of the classroom activities for which you should teach specific directions:

- When students arrive in the morning
- When you are lecturing to the class
- When students enter the classroom after recess
- When students need to go to the rest room
- When students want a drink of water
- When students move from one activity to another
- When it is time for recess
- When the class goes to the school library
- When the fire bell rings
- When the class goes to a school assembly
- When students are in the cafeteria
- When it is time to clean up
- When the class is having a class discussion
- When students are working in cooperative groups
- When students are working with a partner
- When students are taking a test
- When a visitor enters the room
- When students leave at the end of the day

Guidelines for determining specific directions:

Use these guidelines when determining the specific directions for each classroom activity:

- Choose no more than four specific directions for each class activity.
- Your directions must be observable and easy for students to follow. Don't include vague directions such as "act good" or "behave appropriately."
- Relate your directions to:

  —how you want students to participate in the activity or procedure—what you expect them to do.

  —how you expect students to behave in order to be successful in the activity—whether students should be in or out of their seats, whether talking is permitted, whether raising hands is expected.

Examples of specific directions:

When students are working independently at their desks:

1. Have all necessary books, paper, pencils and other materials on your desk.
2. Begin working on your assignment as soon as you receive it. *(These directions let students know what they are expected to do.)*
3. No talking. Raise your hand to ask a question. *(This direction lets students know how you expect them to behave.)*

When students enter the classroom:

1. Walk into the room.
2. Begin working on the assignments listed on the board. *(These directions let students know what they are expected to do.)*
3. No talking after the bell rings. *(This direction lets students know how they are expected to behave.)*

Teach Specific Directions to Students

Ensure that students are successful in following directions by teaching them the specific behaviors you expect. Reteach and review your expectations until every student follows them successfully. The more time you spend at the beginning of the year teaching your specific directions, the less time you'll spend *repeating* them as the year goes by.

Follow these steps for teaching specific directions:

Write your directions on a flipchart.

List all steps for following a direction on a flipchart or posterboard.

Explain the rationale for the direction.

Discuss why it is important for all students to respond to the direction in the same manner.

Explain each step to students.

Explain and demonstrate each behavior listed on the chart. (With younger students, discuss what each behavior "looks like," "sounds like" and "feels like.")

Check for understanding.

Have students explain and demonstrate each behavior.

Give practice in following the direction.

Conduct the actual activity for the directions you've just presented. For example, if you've just given directions for an independent assignment, give an actual assignment to students. Be sure to give plenty of praise for students following the direction successfully.

Keep the directions in view for students the first few times the activity is conducted.

Use Positive Recognition to Motivate Students to Behave

Begin immediately recognizing students for making responsible behavioral choices. Let students know by your words and actions that you are following through with the positives you spoke about when you taught them your classroom discipline plan. When students know that you notice and appreciate the good efforts they're making, they will be more motivated to continue behaving appropriately.

Use the following positive recognition techniques to encourage appropriate behavior and reinforce it.

Positive Repetition

After giving a direction, immediately look for at least two students who are following the direction. Say the students' names and restate the direction while they are following it.

Direction: *"Line up quickly and quietly."*

Positive Repetition: *"Kerri is in line. That was very fast! Sam, you lined up without a sound. Great!"*

Consistent Praise

Continually monitor the class—even while teaching—and provide frequent praise and positive support to on-task students.

Give praise that is:

- Personal. Always include the student's name.
- Genuine. Be genuinely appreciative of the appropriate behavior.
- Specific. State the appropriate behavior.

  "Chris, you waited so quietly while I was speaking to Mrs. Spence. I really appreciate your patience."

Scanning

When you are working with an individual student or with a small group, look up every few minutes and scan the room. Praise students who are on task and behaving appropriately. Students will enjoy the recognition and realize that you are aware of their behavior even when you're not working directly with them.

Circulating the Room

While students are busy working independently, circulate the room and compliment them on their good behavior and work habits. This positive recognition is given quietly—a special message from you to your students.

Redirect Nondisruptive Off-Task Behavior

By giving your students consistent positive recognition, you can prevent the majority of problems before they even begin. However, there still will be students who behave inappropriately. One form of inappropriate behavior is nondisruptive off-task behavior.

Examples of Nondisruptive Off-task Behaviors

- Looking out the window
- Reading instead of listening
- Doodling instead of working

For nondisruptive off-task behavior, use redirecting techniques to provide an opportunity for the student to choose appropriate behavior and return to task:

The Look

Give the off-task student a look that says, *"I'm aware of and disapprove of your behavior."* Maintain eye contact until the student is back on task.

Physical Proximity

Simply walk over and stand close by the student. The student will know why you're there and will know to get back on task.

Mention the off-task student's name while teaching.

When you notice a student who is not paying attention while you're teaching the class, just mention the student's name in the context of your lesson to redirect his or her attention back to task:

"...so, as you can see, Curtis, in this problem, the average age of the group members does not match the actual age of any member of the group."

Proximity Praise

To get an off-task student back on task, praise one or more on-task students in close proximity to the student. When the off-task student looks around and notices what's going on, he or she will be motivated to get back on task.

Use Consequences for Disruptive or Continual Off-Task Behavior

When students are disruptive, or continue to exhibit off-task behavior after you've used redirecting techniques, it is time to implement consequences from your discipline hierarchy.

Examples of Disruptive Behaviors

- Shouting out in class
- Throwing paper airplanes
- Pushing or shoving

Follow these guidelines to ensure that your use of disciplinary consequences will help students choose responsible behavior.

Provide consequences in a calm, matter-of-fact manner.

Because you've planned in advance how you will react to student misbehavior, you will be able to give consequences calmly, without anger and with the assuredness that the consequence is both appropriate and fair.

Be consistent. Provide a consequence every time a student chooses to disrupt.

Your consistency in providing consequences is the key to reducing the amount of disruptive behavior.

Keep a record of all warnings and consequences given throughout the day.

Use the Discipline Log provided on the weekly planning pages in this book to track consequences. Record the specific details of behavior problems on the Behavior Documentation Record on page 103.

After a student receives a consequence, recognize positive behavior at the first opportunity.

After imposing a consequence, look for *appropriate* behavior and provide positive recognition at the first available opportunity.

Nice Improvement!

Provide an "escape mechanism" for students who are upset and want to talk about what happened.

Students often want a chance to tell their side of the story after receiving a consequence. Provide the following "escape mechanisms" to help defuse their anger and "get something off their chest" without disrupting the rest of the class:

- Have the student fill out a "Behavior Journal" sheet that asks the student to reflect upon and explain what happened, and determine alternative behaviors he or she could have chosen.

- Have the student write you a note that you will discuss with him or her after class or when you have a break in the lesson.

- Use a notebook to record misbehavior that allows space for students to write their comments.

Use "moving in" and "moving out" techniques.

When a student continues to disrupt after receiving consequences, "move in" or "move out" to stop disruptive behavior (see guidelines on page 61).

Refocus argumentative conversations.

When a student tries to manipulate you or argue with you, you must stay in charge and *refocus* the conversation. Do not get involved in a pointless argument. Use the Broken Record technique described on page 63 to refocus the conversation to clear behavioral expectations.

Note: For a student who, despite your efforts, is chronically disruptive and does not respond to your classroom discipline plan, it will be necessary to use a more individualized approach. See "Strategies for Dealing with Difficult Students," pages 97-98.

7 REVIEW ASSERTIVE DISCIPLINE GUIDELINES

Review the guidelines for utilizing Assertive Discipline. Refer to Lee Canter's *Assertive Discipline* text and workbooks for additional information on teaching appropriate behavior, preventing problem behavior, and effectively dealing with behavior problems when they arise.

Beginning-of-the-Year Checklist

Before the first week of school.

Take some time to be sure that you have determined your classroom rules, positives and consequences, plus all of the management tasks listed below. You will find that your discipline problems will be greatly reduced when you have done this preparation.

Check off each task as it is completed.

☐ Prepare classwide and individual positive recognition systems.

☐ Prepare positive notes to send home.

☐ Prepare introductory letter to parents (include your classroom discipline plan.)

☐ Prepare a large poster listing your plan, with rules, positives and consequences.

☐ Prepare to share your plan with your principal.

The first day of school.

Set a positive tone in your classroom from the very first day.

Check off each item as it is completed.

☐ Greet students at the door.

☐ Teach your plan to students.

☐ Praise every student.

The first weeks of school.

Your general classroom rules will be in effect at all times. The first rule, "Follow directions," is an important rule in your classroom discipline plan. During the first weeks of school you must continually determine specific directions for each classroom situation and then teach these directions to your students.

Check off each situation below as you teach the specific directions for them.

In-class situations

☐ Lecture

☐ Small groups

☐ Independent work time

☐ Transitions

☐ Getting materials

☐ How to seek help if teacher is busy

☐ Entering and leaving class

☐ What to do when finished early

☐ Pencil sharpening

☐ Lunch

☐ Putting away materials

Out-of-class situations

☐ Halls

☐ Cafeteria

☐ Yard

☐ Library

☐ Before school

☐ After school

☐ Recess (elementary)

Year-at-a-Glance
Guide to Assertive Discipline

SEPTEMBER	• Create a discipline plan. Post in classroom. • Communicate plan to administrator. • Communicate plan to parents. • Teach plan to students. • Prepare discipline plan for substitutes.	**FEBRUARY**	• Hold one-to-one problem-solving conferences with difficult students. • Develop individualized behavior plans. • Promote leadership this month. • Encourage giving to others around Valentine's Day.
OCTOBER	• Explain behavior expectations at Back-to-School Night. • Begin positive communication with parents. • Contact parents at the first sign of a problem. • Document problem behavior. • Build relationships with students.	**MARCH**	• Greet students at the door. • Utilize classwide positives. • Hold problem-solving conferences with parents. • Reach out to unsupportive parents. • Review schoolwide rules with students.
NOVEMBER	• Be consistent in using positives and consequences. • Enlist parent support at parent conferences. • Thank parents, administrator and classroom helpers for their support. • Team up with other teachers for problem-solving of misbehavior.	**APRIL**	• Encourage students to praise each other. • Post a student-recognition bulletin board. • Thank administrator for his or her support. • Call a difficult student after a bad day.
DECEMBER	• Plan special positives for holiday time. • Have students make a "wish list" of positives. • Keep up with behavior documentation. • Hold one-to-one problem-solving conferences with students having problems.	**MAY**	• Reward students with outdoor lessons and activities. • Praise every student at least once a day. • Have parents provide positives and consequences to motivate their child. • Enforce your plan to the very last day of school.
JANUARY	• Assess your plan—make changes, set goals. • Inform your administrator of changes in your plan. • Review behavior expectations with students. • Keep up positive communication with parents.	**JUNE**	• Present recognition awards to students. • Send notes to parents thanking them for their support. • Complete the End-of-the-Year Checklist on page 99. • Complete the Ideas to Use Again chart on pages 100-101.

Long-Range Planning Units

	Subject: _____	Subject: _____	Subject: _____	Subject: _____	Subject: _____
SEPTEMBER					
OCTOBER					
NOVEMBER					
DECEMBER					
JANUARY					

Long-Range Planning Units

	Subject: _____	Subject: _____	Subject: _____	Subject: _____	Subject: _____
FEBRUARY					
MARCH					
APRIL					
MAY					
JUNE					

NAME: WEEK BEGINNING:

SUBJECT:			
M			
T	Praise is the key to good discipline.		
W			
T			
F			

14

		NOTES:
Make sure all rules are observable.		

Introduce Your Discipline Plan

Plan ample time on the first day of school to present and explain your discipline plan to students. After introducing the plan, play a "pop quiz" game to review rules, positives and consequences: Periodically stop what you're doing and pop a question, such as, "What are our five classroom rules?" or "What happens the second time you break a rule?" or "If you have two checks one day, what happens the next day?" Award stickers, stamps or small treats for correct answers.

Set a Positive Tone

Letting students know you care is the single most important action you can take to deter behavior problems. Use these first-day tips:

- Place a welcome note on each student's desk.
- Greet students at the door.
- Share your enthusiasm for activities planned.
- Express interest and concern for every student.
- Praise students for listening to first-day instructions.
- Phone students (later that evening) who have had problems in the past to commend them for a great first day.

Student Discipline Log

_____

_____

_____

_____

_____

_____

_____

_____

NAME: WEEK BEGINNING:

SUBJECT:			
M			
T	Praise each student each day.		
W			
T			
F			

16

		NOTES:
Make sure your rules are clearly posted.		

Introductory Letter to Parents

Send a letter home to parents expressing your commitment to their children, conveying your enthusiasm for an exciting and rewarding year, and sharing some of the goals you hope to achieve as their child's teacher. Also, explain your discipline plan and provide a detachable sign-off sheet so parents can verify that they have read and understand your plan.

Marbles in a Jar

Begin your classwide positive recognition program with this classic technique. Over the years, Marbles in a Jar has proven to be a great positive reinforcer. It's simple, versatile, and extremely effective in motivating appropriate behavior. Simply drop a marble into a jar whenever one or more students behave, or when the whole class is following directions. When the jar is filled, reward the class with a special activity. (See page 94 for variations.)

Student Discipline Log

_____
_____
_____
_____
_____
_____
_____
_____
_____
_____
_____
_____
_____
_____

NAME: WEEK BEGINNING:

SUBJECT:			
M			
T	Greet students with a positive comment.		
W			
T			
F			

18

		NOTES:

Clearly communicate your expectations to students.

Teaching Behavior— A Top Priority

It's one thing for students to know what your classroom rules are. It's another for them to understand exactly what the rules mean. Plan a lesson to teach rules just as you would teach any other subject or skill:

- Clearly state the expectation.
- Describe what the behavior "looks like" and "sounds like."
- Check for understanding by asking students to describe and demonstrate the behavior.
- Provide practice by having the whole class demonstrate the behavior.
- Praise students for a job well done.

ALL ABOUT ME

Someday I want to:

fly my own private plane.

Interest Inventories

The better you know your students, the more effective you will be in motivating them and providing positive recognition. Have students complete a questionnaire that inquires about their "favorites" (books, movies, food) and asks them to share feelings about school, points of view on social issues, personal interests and aspirations. This information will also help you open up more positive communication with students that conveys the message, "I care about you."

Student Discipline Log

_____

_____

_____

_____

_____

_____

_____

NAME: WEEK BEGINNING:

SUBJECT:			
M			
T	The key to success is consistency.		
W			
T			
F			

		NOTES:
Be specific when giving praise.		

Specific Directions Flipchart

When introducing a new set of directions, list them on a large flipchart and keep them in view for students the first few times you conduct the activity. For example:

Directions for a Math Quiz

1. Clear desk except for a pencil.
2. Stay in seat, no talking.
3. Raise hand if you have a question.

By referring to the flipchart, students will be more successful in following directions and as a result, you will have more opportunity to praise them.

★ JAN
RAMON
CINDY
LEAH
NANCY
BERT

Star Box

A subtle gesture is often all it takes to motivate on-task students to *stay* on task and encourage off-task students to *get* on task. During your lesson, walk up to the chalkboard, look around the room, and without saying anything, write the names of on-task students in a "star box" drawn on the board. At the end of the day present Star Student Awards to students whose names are in the box.

Student Discipline Log

_____

_____

_____

_____

_____

_____

_____

_____

_____

NAME: WEEK BEGINNING:

SUBJECT:			
M			
T	Take time to teach directions.		
W			
T			
F			

		NOTES:
Use minimal consequences.		

Make a Few Special Phone Calls

Do you have students in your class who have a history of behavior problems? Reverse the cycle of failure by making your first communication to the student's home a positive one. Phone the parents to let them know you will do everything possible to turn things around for their child this year. Ask for their input, and assure them that by working together their child will have more success at school. When a problem arises, parents will be more willing to give their support because they know you care about their child.

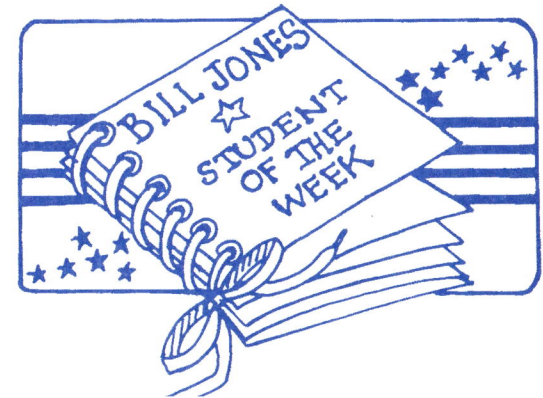

Student of the Week

High self-esteem is the cornerstone of good behavior. Institute a Student of the Week activity early in the year to build self-esteem and give special recognition to students. Each week, honor a student by:

- Having the student display favorite photos and personal items.
- Asking parents to write a heartwarming letter to their child. Read it to the class.
- Having classmates write complimentary notes.
- Photographing the student in a self-created pose.
- Mounting the photo, notes and letter in a Student-of-the-Week keepsake album.

Student Discipline Log

_____
_____
_____
_____
_____
_____
_____

NAME: WEEK BEGINNING:

SUBJECT:			
M			
T	Get to know your students.		
W			
T			
F			

24

		NOTES:
Use classwide positive recognition activities.		

Boost Back-to-School Night Attendance

You've put a lot of time into preparing your Back-to-School Night presentation. But it will be effective only if parents show up to hear what you have to say. In addition to sending invitations, ensure an excellent turnout by phoning parents the night before the event to say that you have an exciting evening in store for them and will be sharing important information and special activities you've planned for their child. When parents arrive, stress the importance of teaming up for their child's success, and thank them for showing their support by attending.

Help Wanted

Eliminate the need for students to get out of their seats, raise their hands wildly or call out to you for help on an assignment. Have students make Help Wanted signs using Tinker Toys®, tagboard, and a piece of packing tape. When help is needed, the student puts out his or her Help Wanted sign and quietly waits for help to arrive from you, a classroom aide, parent volunteer or classmate who has finished early.

Student Discipline Log

_____
_____
_____
_____
_____
_____
_____
_____

NAME: WEEK BEGINNING:

SUBJECT:			
M			
T	Document all problem behaviors.		
W			
T			
F			

		NOTES:
Give praise that is genuine and sincere.		

Nonverbal Reinforcers

For many students, a smile or a hug from you can be the most meaningful motivator for good behavior. Enhance your repertiore of positive recognition techniques with these simple nonverbal gestures:

- Look the student in the eye and smile.
- Give a thumbs up or a "high five."
- Wink or nod to express approval.
- Give a hug about shoulder level.
- Offer a handshake for a job well done.
- Write a compliment on students' work.
- Give a gentle pat on the back.

(Be sure to continue the positive strategies presented on pages 8 and 94-96.)

Silent Reminders

Every student can benefit from a reminder now and then to choose good behavior. Have students make their own "silent reminders":

- a "Follow directions" pencil topper.
- a "Bring all materials to class" supply-box label.
- a desktop sign with all five rules on it.

Student Discipline Log

_____

_____

_____

_____

_____

_____

_____

_____

_____

_____

NAME: WEEK BEGINNING:

SUBJECT:			
M			
T	Build positive relationships with parents.		
W			
T			
F			

		NOTES:

Use positive recognition to prevent behavior problems.

Use an Assertive Response Style

How you respond to misbehavior is critical to your behavior management success. The most effective response is an assertive one—a calm, firm communication to the student that clearly states the desired behavior (without attacking him or her personally): *"Ben, the rule in our classroom is 'Keep hands and feet to yourself.'"* Avoid nonassertive responses, such as, *"How many times do I have to tell you to follow directions?"* and hostile responses, *"It's about time you did something right."* These serve neither the student's best interest nor yours.

Brag Box

Have students decorate an empty facial tissue box to create their own "brag box." When you notice a student's good efforts, drop a note of praise into his or her box. Encourage students to deposit complimentary messages into each others' boxes as well. At the end of the week students remove and share their notes, staple them together, and attach a cover sheet that reads, for example, *Kate's Brag Box Messages*. Make sure students bring them home to share with parents.

Student Discipline Log

_____
_____
_____
_____
_____
_____
_____
_____
_____

SUBJECT:			
M			
T	Praise students who follow directions.		
W			
T			
F			

		NOTES:

Use redirecting techniques to increase time on task.

Positive Communication with Parents

Parents enjoy hearing about their child's good efforts at school. Unfortunately, many parents hear from school only when there is a problem. Establish yearlong positive communication with parents by sending home positive notes and making positive phone calls (even to parents with shared custody). Plan to make two positive contacts a day. Within a month you'll have reached the parents of every student in your class. Parents who see that you care about their children will be more supportive, even when there is a problem.

Class Photo Album

Keep a loaded camera handy and use it throughout the year to photograph students behaving appropriately (while working individually, as partners or in cooperative groups). Use these photos to create a class photo album. Keep it on display in your classroom for students, parents and visitors to peruse. At the end of the year, there should be several photos of each student. Send them home with praise-filled notes to parents.

Student Discipline Log

_____
_____
_____
_____
_____
_____
_____
_____
_____
_____

NAME: WEEK BEGINNING:

SUBJECT:			
M			
T	Let students know you care.		
W			
T			
F			

32

		NOTES:
Promote positive peer relationships.		

Parent-Conference Extras

A parent conference is not only an opportunity to report academic progress, but to gain parents' confidence and support as well:

Relate experiences that highlight students' strengths: *"Bill was a great sport and natural leader last week when our class lost the championship volleyball game. He initiated a handshake lineup between the two teams. I was very impressed."*

Ask questions that convey the importance you place on the home-school partnership: *"What would you like to see happen with your child this year? What concerns do you have regarding your child? What can I do to make this a rewarding year for your child?"*

Cards for All Occasions

Building relationships with students is key in preventing behavior problems. Nurture your relationships by surprising students with birthday greetings, get-well cards, thank-you notes, and cards that simply say you think they're terrific. Purchase an economical box of all-occasion cards at a flea market or yard sale, or pick up a card or two every now and then at the grocery store. Always include your own personal message on pre-printed cards.

Student Discipline Log

_____

_____

_____

_____

_____

_____

_____

NAME: WEEK BEGINNING:

SUBJECT:			
M			
T	Respond to students in a calm, caring manner.		
W			
T			
F			

		NOTES:
Send home two positive notes today.		

The Choice Is Theirs

It is your students' responsibility to choose appropriate behavior. Your job is to encourage good choices:

- Present consequences as a choice: *"Jen, you have a choice: sit down now, or we will call your mom after class."*

- Help students see that it is they who determine the outcomes of their choices: *"Ron, you chose to stay after class, and I can see that you're not pleased with your choice. Let's talk about what you can do differently next time."*

- Help students recognize their good choices: *"Juan, I know how hard it was to walk away when Tim was teasing you. It took a lot of courage, but you made the right choice."*

Lucky Stars

Conduct a weekly raffle to recognize students' shining behavior. Create a stockpile of yellow stars. Allow students who begin work promptly and stay on task to write their name on one of the stars and drop it into a jar. At the end of the week, draw several stars from the jar, announce the "Lucky Star" winners and reward them with fast-food certificates donated by local merchants.

Student Discipline Log

_____

_____

_____

_____

_____

_____

_____

_____

_____

NAME: WEEK BEGINNING:

SUBJECT:			
M			
T	Make one positive phone call home.		
W			
T			
F			

		NOTES:
Contact parents at the first sign of a problem.		

Show Your Appreciation

The adults in your school community enjoy positive recognition as much as students do. Use Thanksgiving time as an opportunity to thank those who have helped to make the first few months of school successful and rewarding for you and your students. Send notes of appreciation to parents, your administrator and the PTA for their support, to classroom helpers for their time and dedication, and to your students for giving you their attention and best efforts in the classroom.

Boast-It Notes

Find something in every student to boast about. Keep a small pad of self-stick notes in your pocket. Throughout the day look for students who are making responsible choices. Recognize their efforts by writing a few complimentary words on the pad (*Jason, you stayed in your seat during math. Great job!*). Peel off the note and stick it onto the student's desk, cubby or shirt sleeve.

Student Discipline Log

_____
_____
_____
_____
_____
_____
_____
_____
_____
_____
_____
_____
_____
_____

NAME: WEEK BEGINNING:

SUBJECT:			
M			
T	Special privileges make great motivators.		
W			
T			
F			

		NOTES:
Model a positive attitude.		

Use the "Your Own Child" Test

Parents' most common complaint is that teachers wait too long before contacting them about a problem at school. To determine whether it's appropriate to contact parents regarding a behavioral or academic problem, use the "your own child" test. Simply ask yourself, "If this were my child, would I want to hear from the teacher?" By thinking as a parent for a moment, it will become clear that contact should be made more often than not.

Student Hotline

Recognition and approval from parents is essential in building student self-esteem and motivation. When a student exhibits noteworthy behavior, allow him or her to join you during lunch or recess to phone home and share the good news with parents. First explain to parents why you're calling and generate their enthusiasm. Then let the student give the exciting details. If you reach an answering machine, leave your messages just the same. Parents will be delighted to hear them when they return home from their busy day.

Student Discipline Log

_____
_____
_____
_____
_____
_____
_____
_____
_____
_____

SUBJECT:			
M			
T	Positively support aides and volunteers.		
W			
T			
F			

		NOTES:
Focus on students' strenghts.		

Redirecting Techniques

Oftentimes students stray off task but are not disruptive (daydreaming, head on desk). Teachers often ignore this type of behavior or they issue a consequence. Ignoring gives the student license to not learn. Consequences should be reserved for disruptive or continual off-task behavior. Use redirecting techniques to get nondisruptive off-task students back on task:

- The Look: Give the student a look that says, "I'm aware of and disapprove of your behavior."

- Physical Proximity: Stand next to the student while teaching.

- Mention the student's name while teaching: "...so, Trevor, we've come up with two possible solutions to Wilbur's problem in this chapter."

- Proximity Praise: Praise an on-task student sitting near the off-task student.

Praise by Mail

Students enjoy receiving mail addressed directly to them. Let students know that when they behave responsibly you will mail them a special letter that they can share with their parents. Create your own "positive" letterhead and duplicate enough sheets to send a praise-filled message to each student in your class.

Student Discipline Log

_____

_____

_____

_____

_____

_____

_____

_____

NAME: WEEK BEGINNING:

SUBJECT:			
M			
T			
W			
T			
F			

Treat students the way you would want your child to be treated.

		NOTES:
Plan special positives for holiday time.		

Document Problem Behavior

Consistent, factual behavior documentation is essential in obtaining support from parents, administrators and special services. When a warning is given, jot the student's name on a clipboard. Then, put a check next to it for each consequence imposed thereafter. At the end of the day, log behavior problems on individual student documentation sheets:

- Note the date and time the problem occurred.
- Describe the problem behavior in detail—just facts, no value judgments.
- List actions taken with the student, parent contact made, and follow-up actions to be taken.

Stocking Stuffers

The first snow, holiday parties and anticipation of winter vacation can throw any student off the good-behavior track. This is a good time to step up your behavior management efforts. Display a holiday stocking filled with certificates that entitle students to special privileges (selecting own seat for the day, teacher's assistant, a holiday art activity). Present the certificates to students who behave appropriately during this exciting time of year.

Student Discipline Log

_____

_____

_____

_____

_____

_____

_____

_____

_____

_____

SUBJECT:			
M			
T			
W			
T			
F			

Express confidence in students' ability to make good choices.

		NOTES:
Positively support your administrator.		

How Are You Doing?

The beginning of the new year is a good time to assess your discipline plan, make necessary changes and set new goals. Ask yourself:

- Am I consistent in enforcing my plan?
- Are students following my rules and directions?
- Are students responding to my positives and consequences?
- Are there students who need more positive attention?
- Am I making enough positive phone calls to parents?
- Have I contacted parents to resolve problems?
- Is there a problem time of the day that needs to be dealt with more effectively?
- Are there students with whom I need to work on our relationship?

Snowball Mural

As the weather turns colder and students spend more time indoors, behavior problems are likely to erupt. Combat misbehavior caused by cabin fever by distributing "snowballs" (white cotton balls) to students who behave. Students store their snowballs in resealable bags. At the end of two weeks, reward the class with a winter art activity: students use their snowballs to create a classroom mural of a snowy scene.

Student Discipline Log

_____

_____

_____

_____

_____

_____

_____

_____

NAME: WEEK BEGINNING:

SUBJECT:			
M			
T	Let parents know you care about their child.		
W			
T			
F			

		NOTES:
Review your expectations with students.		

Transitions

Transitions can be difficult. Valuable time is often lost, behavior problems occur and the room becomes noisy and disorderly. Follow these steps to prepare students for a smooth transition:

First, give clear instructions for how students are to move from one activity to the next. Tell students not to begin until you give the signal.

Second, introduce a signal that requires students' attention (e.g., thumb in the air).

Third, have several students demonstrate the steps you've taught.

Finally, give the signal to the entire class. Praise students for a smooth transition.

Instant Credit

Encourage students to seat themselves and settle down as soon as they enter your room by awarding Instant Credit Coupons. Each time the entire class is seated and ready by the time the bell rings—in the morning, or after lunch, recess, or a transition—post an Instant Credit Coupon on the board. After 10 coupons are earned, reward the class with free time, music in class or a special snack.

Student Discipline Log

_____

_____

_____

_____

_____

_____

_____

_____

_____

_____

NAME: WEEK BEGINNING:

SUBJECT:			
M			
T	If your discipline plan is not working, change it.		
W			
T			
F			

48

		NOTES:
Design a positive recognition bulletin board.		

Time Away

Time away from others stops disruptions and helps students regain control of their behavior. Choose from three variations of this strategy:

Change the student's seat when he is disturbing a classmate. Require participation in the lesson.

Move the student away from the group if she is overstimulated, upset or angry. Allow the student to return when she feels ready.

Move the student to another classroom when he continually disrupts the class (pre-arrange with neighboring teacher) and have him complete work there.

During a "Time Away," have students complete a Think Sheet (page 51). Afterwards, meet with the student to express your concern and refocus on the positive.

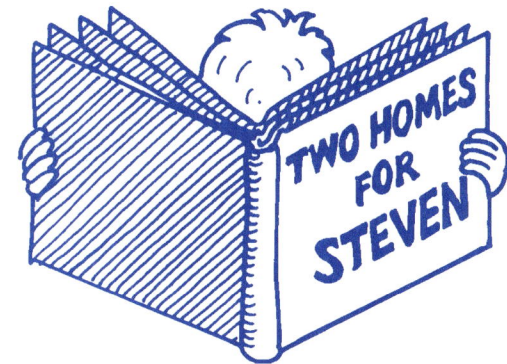

Bonus Books

Behavior problems at school often stem from issues students face outside of school (divorce, loss of a loved one, new baby, step-relatives, domestic violence, substance abuse). Establish a classroom library of books that help students deal with such issues. Offer them to individuals, or use as springboards to classwide discussions and writing activities. You may be the only adult in some students' lives who is actively helping them develop a sense of hope.

Student Discipline Log

_____
_____
_____
_____
_____
_____
_____
_____

SUBJECT:			
M			
T			
W			
T			
F			

After a consequence, find an opportunity to praise the student.

		NOTES:
Involve your principal in positive recognition of students.		

The Think Sheet

After a conflict between students or a disruptive outburst in class, have the student(s) fill out a Think Sheet to reflect on what happened and determine appropriate alternative behaviors. Include the following on the Think Sheet:

- This is the rule I broke:
- I chose to break this rule because:
- Who was bothered when I broke this rule?
- This is what I could have done instead:

Discuss the student's responses and express your confidence in his or her ability to make appropriate choices in the future.

Desktop Motivators

On a sheet of paper, draw a simple game board (pirate searching for buried treasure, lost puppy finding its way home). Tape a copy to each student's desk. Reinforce good behavior by praising students and putting your initials in the first (or next available) section along the game-board path. The student colors each initialed section. When all sections are colored, allow the student to lead a classroom game.

Student Discipline Log

_____

_____

_____

_____

_____

_____

_____

_____

_____

NAME: WEEK BEGINNING:

SUBJECT:			
M			
T			
W			
T			
F			

Do not wait for parent conferences to discuss problems.

		NOTES:
Praise students during transition time.		

Plan for Latecomers

When a new student enters your class, assign him or her a class buddy who will:

- explain your classroom discipline plan and specific directions.
- give the new student a tour of the school.
- explain schoolwide rules for the cafeteria and yard.
- help the new student develop friendships.
- be available to answer questions during and after the school day.

Give plenty of praise to both students for their congenial efforts.

Conversation Hearts

Purchase one or two bags of candy conversation hearts. When praising individuals or groups of students, drop a few hearts into a heart-shaped box or vase. When all of the hearts are deposited, enjoy a sweet celebration of student success. Divide the hearts among students, pour some red punch or fruit juice, and hand-deliver to each student a special valentine from you!

Student Discipline Log

_____
_____
_____
_____
_____
_____
_____
_____
_____
_____
_____

NAME: WEEK BEGINNING:

SUBJECT:			
M			
T	Catch 'em being good.		
W			
T			
F			

		NOTES:
Encourage students to praise each other.		

Homework Tips for Parents

Most parents want to help their child become more responsible with homework but often don't know how. Send home a list of tips that will help parents to be more supportive of your homework efforts:

- Set up a quiet, well-lit study area for your child.
- Schedule and enforce daily homework time.
- Create a box of supplies needed for homework.
- Encourage your child to work independently.
- Check to see that homework is completed.
- Establish a spot for depositing completed work to be returned to school.
- Contact the teacher if you have concerns.

Homework Extension Coupons

Provide motivation for students to meet your homework expectations by presenting Homework Extension coupons to those who complete all homework for one week, turn in homework on time, or demonstrate other responsible homework habits you're looking for. Students redeem their coupons to gain an extra day to turn in a homework assignment of their choice.

Student Discipline Log

_____
_____
_____
_____
_____
_____
_____
_____
_____
_____

NAME: WEEK BEGINNING:

SUBJECT:			
M			
T	Build relationships with difficult students.		
W			
T			
F			

		NOTES:
Encourage good behavioral choices.		

When a Sub Is in the Room

Ensure good behavior during your absence. In addition to leaving a copy of your discipline plan and detailed lessons for a sub, leave "While You Were Away" sheets for students to complete. Instruct the substitute to have each student list ten responsible behaviors they demonstrated while you were away. When you return, have students share their lists. Be sure to give plenty of praise for their cooperation.

GOLD CARD					
Mrs. Jay	P.J.	B.J.	B.J.		
Miss Aaron	SA	SA	SA	SA	
Mr. Emilio	TE	TE	TE		
Mrs. Irving	J.I.	J.I.	J.I.	J.I.	J.I.

Gold Cards

Team up with fellow teachers to positively support students who are having behavior problems. Distribute "Gold Cards" which list the names of the teachers that work with the student (math, speech, music, p.e., art, special ed.). Provide a row of five boxes next to each name. Students carry their Gold Cards from class to class. Teachers initial one of the boxes in their row when the student is "caught" making good choices. When all boxes on the card are initialed, the student receives a reward or privilege, and a special "congratulations" from his or her teachers.

Student Discipline Log

_____
_____
_____
_____
_____
_____
_____
_____
_____
_____
_____

NAME: WEEK BEGINNING:

SUBJECT:			
M			
T	Monitor students' behavior in the cafeteria.		
W			
T			
F			

		NOTES:
Send home classroom newsletters.		

A Matter of Trust

Students who refuse to meet behavioral expectations at school often lack trust in their teachers. Use these two simple strategies for building trust and positive relationships with these students:

Phone the student after a bad day. In a caring manner, express that you feel bad about the difficult time you both had. Listen to what the student has to say and assure him or her that tomorrow will be a better day.

Phone the student after a good day. Let the student know you noticed the terrific effort he or she has made. Stress how much you appreciate the improvement.

1 Free Time
2 Line Leader
3 Choose Seat

A Roll of the Dice

Post a list of six positives and number them with number six being the most desired treat or privilege. Students who are "caught" behaving appropriately earn a chance to roll a die to determine which positive they will receive.

Student Discipline Log

_____
_____
_____
_____
_____
_____
_____
_____
_____
_____
_____
_____
_____

NAME: WEEK BEGINNING:

SUBJECT:			
M			
T	Circulate the room and praise students.		
W			
T			
F			

		NOTES:
Meet with students to solve problems.		

"Moving In" and "Moving Out"

When a student continues to disrupt after you've given consequences, use "moving in" and "moving out" techniques to stop the disruptive behavior and encourage appropriate choices:

Move In. Calmly walk up to the student, look him in the eye, and in a concerned, quiet, firm manner tell him his behavior is inappropriate. Clearly state your expectation and what will happen next if misbehavior continues.

Move Out. Move to the hallway or corner of the room away from the student's audience of peers to have your talk (as outlined above). Stay calm and recognize her feelings.

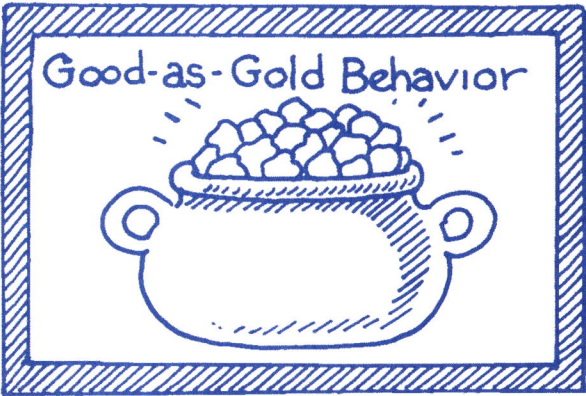

Good-as-Gold Behavior

Pot O' Gold

Cut out a large construction-paper tureen and post it on a "Pot O' Gold" bulletin board. Then, using yellow paper or gold foil, cut out 20-25 gold nuggets. Positively reinforce appropriate behavior, individually and classwide, by posting gold nuggets "in the pot." When a predetermined number of nuggets is posted, reward each student with a gold-foil-wrapped chocolate coin.

Student Discipline Log

_____
_____
_____
_____
_____
_____
_____
_____
_____

NAME: WEEK BEGINNING:

SUBJECT:			
M			
T	Begin the day on a positive note.		
W			
T			
F			

		NOTES:
Share good news with parents.		

The Broken-Record Technique

Don't be lured into the sidetracking tactics of argumentative students. Use the Broken Record technique to refocus the conversation back to clear behavioral expectations.

Teacher: *You need to sit down and do your work.*

Student: *I'm not bothering anyone. You're not being fair!*

Teacher: *I understand that you feel like walking around, but you need to sit down in your seat and do your work.*

Student: *Why are you always getting me in trouble? I didn't do anything.*

Teacher: *Nick, I see that you're upset, but sit down and begin working. If you choose not to follow directions, you and I will call your mom at work.*

COOPERATION

Letter by Letter

Promote cooperation in your classroom. Display the word "cooperation" in large letters. Throughout the day, discuss and encourage cooperative behavior. When an individual or the whole class cooperates, pin a star over the first (or next available) letter of the word. When the star reaches the last letter, reward students with favorite activities that require cooperation, such as a craft project or an aerobics video.

(Variation: Use this idea to promote responsibility, citizenship or problem-solving.)

Student Discipline Log

_____
_____
_____
_____
_____
_____
_____
_____
_____
_____

NAME: WEEK BEGINNING:

SUBJECT:			
M			
T	Document all misbehavior.		
W			
T			
F			

		NOTES:
Meet with parents to solve problems.		

Be Proactive

Do you feel as though you're so busy putting out fires and dealing with problems that you don't have time to take steps to prevent them? Minimize time spent handling problems by proactively planning on a regular basis how you will maintain a smooth-running classroom. Each week plan in writing:

- which students you will positively recognize.
- which parents you will be writing or phoning.
- how you will build relationships with students.
- steps you will take to solve problems.
- how you will make your lessons more motivating.
- how you will meet students' special needs.
- which tasks you will delegate to students, parent volunteers, and other helpers.

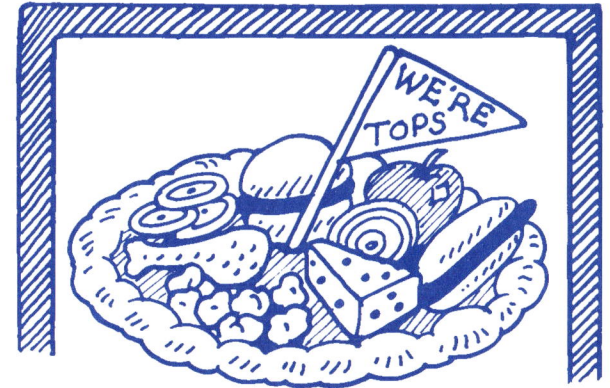

50 Fabulous Toppings

Create a "50 Fabulous Toppings" bulletin board displaying a large picture of a pizza crust. Cut out 50 colorful pictures of food items and put them in a "toppings tray." Allow students who behave appropriately to add a tasty topping to the pizza. When all 50 toppings are posted, treat the class to a Friday afternoon pizza party (sponsored by donations from parents or a local business).

Student Discipline Log

_____
_____
_____
_____
_____
_____
_____
_____
_____

NAME: WEEK BEGINNING:

SUBJECT:			
M			
T	Plan a long-range positive activity.		
W			
T			
F			

		NOTES:
Phone a difficult student after a bad day.		

Review Behavior Expectations

Before and after spring break, students are full of energy and behavior may slip. Plan motivating activities to review expectations with your class:

- Have partners or small groups create role-plays or skits that demonstrate what happens when students follow (or break) classroom rules.

- Invite the principal for an oral presentation of your discipline plan given by students.

- Have cooperative groups create a "Complete Guide to Behavior Expectations in Room 18" pamphlet for visitors and new students.

Greeting Card Factory

Encourage students to positively recognize each other. Stock an area of your classroom with an assortment of art supplies, a dictionary, paper and envelopes for students to create their own greeting cards. When a student feels inspired to send warm wishes to a classmate, teacher, friend or relative, allow him or her to go to the "Greeting Card Factory" to design and write a customized greeting for that special someone—a meaningful way to develop writing skills, creativity and positive relationships.

Student Discipline Log

_____
_____
_____
_____
_____
_____
_____
_____
_____
_____

SUBJECT:			
M			
T	Review the schoolwide rules.		
W			
T			
F			

		NOTES:
Positively recognize supportive parents.		

Be a Facilitator

Your active participation with students helps keep their behavior focused in a positive direction. Hold off sitting at your desk and grading papers until planning period or after school. While students are busy discovering, problem-solving, researching, brainstorming, creating, and applying knowledge, be a facilitator of these processes. Circulate the room and:

- praise students for working cooperatively.
- redirect off-task students.
- recognize students for their ideas.
- suggest additional resources for students.
- help with problem-solving activities.
- assist those needing help.

Celebrations All Year Long

Purchase a few small metallic balloons on sticks (from grocery or drug store) bearing messages such as, "You're Special," or "Time to Celebrate." Create clay stands for the balloons and keep them on a windowsill or countertop. Each day find opportunities to celebrate students' efforts by ceremoniously placing one of the balloons on the student's desk and offering a few heartfelt words about the great job the student is doing.

Student Discipline Log

_____
_____
_____
_____
_____
_____
_____
_____
_____

SUBJECT:			
M			
T	Use classwide positive reinforcement.		
W			
T			
F			

<table>
<tr><td></td><td></td><td>NOTES:</td></tr>
<tr><td></td><td></td><td></td></tr>
<tr><td></td><td></td><td></td></tr>
<tr><td></td><td></td><td></td></tr>
<tr><td>Make a positive phone call home.</td><td></td><td></td></tr>
<tr><td></td><td></td><td></td></tr>
</table>

One-to-One Problem-Solving with Students

You can't solve students' problems outside of school, but you can help them with school-related issues. When a student is having a problem, teach him or her to be solution-oriented. Meet one-to-one and help the student to:

1. Identify the problem.
2. Discuss the student's previous responses to the problem.
3. Identify outcomes produced by previous responses.
4. Determine alternative responses to the problem.

Monitor student's progress and provide follow-up.

Instead of Marbles...

You've been dropping marbles in a jar all year long. It's time for a change. Add a little variety to this activity by replacing the marbles with:

• Peanuts (in the shell)
• Carob-covered malt balls
• Sugarfree lollipops
• Wrapped hard candies
• Tootsie rolls

When the jar is full, distribute the goodies.

Student Discipline Log

_____
_____
_____
_____
_____
_____
_____
_____

NAME: WEEK BEGINNING:

SUBJECT:			
M			
T	Show empathy and concern.		
W			
T			
F			

72

		NOTES:
Support verbal praise with positive notes.		

Audience Behavior

Being an attentive, well-behaved member of an audience is a social skill students need both in and out of school. Before schoolwide assemblies and classroom presentations, give specific directions for how students are expected to behave. After the performance or presentation, have students evaluate how well they exhibited the following good-audience behaviors:

- Walk in line when entering and exiting.
- Sit still.
- No talking.
- Listen attentively.
- Look at the presenter.
- Make appropriate responses—nod, smile, applaud.

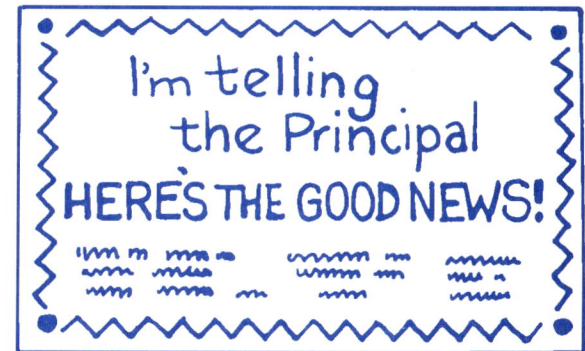

I'm telling
the Principal
HERE'S THE GOOD NEWS!

I'm Telling the Principal!

You've involved your principal in disciplinary actions with students. But have you involved him or her in positive recognition as well? Prepare a stockpile of "I'm Telling the Principal" awards. Just fill in the award with the student's name and a good-behavior message. Then, have the student hand-deliver it to the principal, whom you will have already spoken to about giving plenty of praise to the student and signing his or her award.

Student Discipline Log

NAME: WEEK BEGINNING:

SUBJECT:			
M			
T	Re-evaluate your plan.		
W			
T			
F			

		NOTES:

Inform your administrator of changes in your plan.

Attention Seekers

A student who needs attention will take whatever kind of attention he or she can get from you—positive or negative. Plan to give your attention seekers the maximum amount of positive attention for appropriate behavior, and minimal attention for negative behavior. Use consequences as a last resort. Students will soon learn how best to gain the attention they want.

Stretch, Shake and Wiggle

When you notice students becoming restless take a moment to do a "stretch, shake and wiggle" exercise to give them a short break from the lesson or assignment and enable them to return to task refreshed and ready to work. Ask students to:

1. Stand up, place feet apart, stretch arms up while taking a deep breath, then lower arms while exhaling.

2. Shake their hands, then legs, then whole body.

3. Wiggle their fingers, nose, ears and toes.

4. Take another big breath, exhale, relax, close eyes and visualize how they will get back to work (quickly, quietly, attentively).

Student Discipline Log

_____
_____
_____
_____
_____
_____
_____
_____
_____

NAME: WEEK BEGINNING:

SUBJECT:			
M			
T	Use nonverbal positive reinforcers.		
W			
T			
F			

		NOTES:
Present consequences as a choice.		

Discipline Squad

Form a Discipline Squad for back-up in situations in which a student becomes so verbally abusive or physically hostile that he or she must be removed from the room. A Discipline Squad is comprised of several staff members who can be called upon to escort a student to the office. Meet with your team in advance to discuss procedures for such an occurrence: how they will be signaled, how their classes will be covered and what to do if the principal is out of the building.

Rap Session 2:15 Today

Afternoon Rap

Give students an opportunity to voice concerns on school-related issues and practice problem solving. Each afternoon, hold a 15-minute "rap session" to discuss one issue raised by an individual or a group of students (too much other homework while research projects are due, a student's new set of markers is missing). Set the ground rules: one person speaks at a time; no putdowns or yelling; make only positive suggestions; finish on time. Issues needing further discussion can continue the next day.

Student Discipline Log

_____
_____
_____
_____
_____
_____
_____
_____
_____
_____
_____

SUBJECT:			
M			
T	Involve volunteers in your positive program.		
W			
T			
F			

		NOTES:
Remember that all students can behave.		

Problem Solving with Parents

When problem behavior persists, call parent(s) in for a problem-solving conference. Write down beforehand what you plan to say. Cover the following points:

- Begin with a statement of concern.
- Describe the problem, present documentation and explain what you've already done to solve the problem.
- Ask parents for their suggestions.
- Explain what you will do and what you need the parent to do to solve the problem.
- Express your confidence that working together will help their child succeed.
- Tell parents when you will make follow-up contact.
- Recap the key points of the conference.

Make notes on your conference and file with the student's behavior documentation.

Travel Bag

Keep a collection of travel-size toiletries and sample-size snacks in a duffel bag or backpack (ask for donations from staff, friends and family). Reward well-behaved students with a trip to the travel bag to select a special prize or treat.

Student Discipline Log

_____
_____
_____
_____
_____
_____
_____
_____

NAME: WEEK BEGINNING:

SUBJECT:			
M			
T	Think positively.		
W			
T			
F			

		NOTES:
Clearly communicate your expectations to students.		

Use a Paradoxical Response

When a student is defiant, talks back or refuses to comply with a request, he or she usually expects you to react with anger and ultimatums. Instead, use a paradoxical response: If the student is shouting, speak softly. If the student yells louder, speak more softly still. This technique takes the student off guard and de-escalates the confrontation. It shows the student that you are in control and are staying in control. You are not becoming part of an argument.

Mystery Reward

Use a Mystery Reward to positively reinforce your entire class. Plan an activity that will become your Mystery Reward, for example, "kickball game." Each time one or more students are behaving appropriately, walk to the board and write one letter of your Mystery Reward. When the entire word(s) is written, the students receive the activity… kickball game.

Plan a Mystery Reward for this week in the space below.

Student Discipline Log

_____
_____
_____
_____
_____
_____
_____
_____
_____
_____
_____
_____

NAME: WEEK BEGINNING:

SUBJECT:			
M			
T	Keep parents informed of misbehavior.		
W			
T			
F			

		NOTES:
For behavior to change, you must use positive reinforcement.		

Tips for Team Teachers

If you team teach, you know how important it is to coordinate your behavior management efforts with team members and provide consistency for your students. Use these teaming tips:

- Create your discipline plan together.
- Meet at least once a week to discuss problems and progress in students' behavior.
- Coordinate efforts to positively support students.
- Share the responsibility of making positive calls and write positive notes to parents.
- Join together when problem solving with parents.
- Meet with other teams to share ideas.

No-Homework Night

You used Homework Extension Coupons (page 55) to reward individual students for good behavior and homework habits. Here's an idea for reinforcing the whole class. If all students complete their homework assignments for the week, the entire class is awarded a no-homework night during the following week.

Student Discipline Log

_____
_____
_____
_____
_____
_____
_____
_____
_____
_____
_____
_____

SUBJECT:			
M			
T	Pair positives with praise.		
W			
T			
F			

		NOTES:
Team up with colleagues to solve problems.		

Group Problem-Solving

Next time a problem arises that affects your whole class (chaos at clean-up, not enough art supplies for all students) conduct a group problem-solving session:

First, have students brainstorm solutions. List all suggested solutions on a large sheet of paper.

Second, divide students into small groups to discuss the solutions and agree upon one.

Third, have a member of each group share the group's decision and the rationale behind it.

Fourth, as a class, select a solution to the problem and develop steps to put it into action.

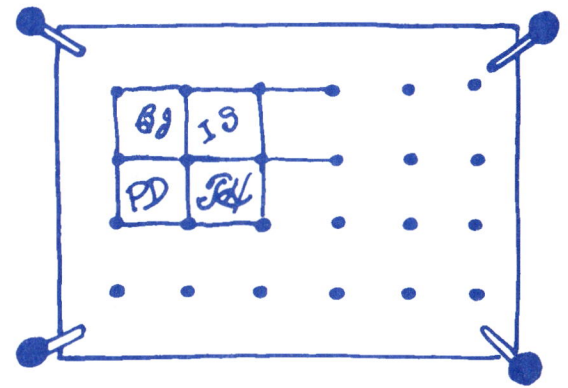

Box Seats

An effective incentive for students to behave is to reward them with the privilege of selecting their own seat for the day. Display a poster consisting of 36 dots, six across, six down. Students who are "caught" being good may draw a horizontal or vertical line connecting two adjacent dots. When a student draws a line that completes a square, the student puts his or her initials in the box and selects a seat of his or her choice for the rest of the day (or the next day).

Student Discipline Log

_____
_____
_____
_____
_____
_____
_____
_____
_____
_____
_____

NAME: WEEK BEGINNING:

SUBJECT:			
M			
T			
W			
T			
F			

Develop individualized behavior plans when necessary.

		NOTES:
Be consistent in following your plan.		

Teacher Assistance Team

One of the most valuable resources teachers have for finding solutions to persistent behavior problems is…each other! Join with colleagues to form a Teacher Assistance Team—a support group that meets every week or two to brainstorm solutions to specific behavior problems. Sharing insights and ideas will help you succeed with challenging students, avoid burnout and experience more success and satisfaction in your job.

Cooperative-Group Logos

Promote camaraderie and cooperation among students. Have cooperative groups design logos symbolizing their group's positive attributes (for example, five hands grasping a light bulb may symbolize that students work together to come up with new ideas). Each group brainstorms logo ideas, creates sketches of possible logo designs, then brings one design to final art. Have each group present their logo to the class and explain how the group's attributes help them to be successful. Make photocopies of each group's logo so they can display them in their work area and on completed work.

Student Discipline Log

_____
_____
_____
_____
_____
_____
_____
_____
_____

SUBJECT:			
M			
T	Instill an "I can do it" attitude in your students.		
W			
T			
F			

Praise specific appropriate behaviors.

Individualized Behavior Plan

Develop individualized behavior plans for students who are not responding to your classroom discipline plan. Include the following:

- Specific behavior(s) required of the student: *Complete class assignments.*

- More motivating positive reinforcement: *Receive one point for each completed assignment. When five points are earned, take class pet home overnight.*

- Stronger, more meaningful consequences: *Each day assignments are not completed, parents are called and TV privileges taken away.*

- Relationship-building strategies: *Spend 5-10 minutes one-to-one time each day.*

Popcorn Positives

Display a large picture of a bowl. Cut out construction paper pieces of popcorn. Choose a behavior the class needs to work on (arriving to class on time, working quietly, keeping their desk area clean). Each time you see one or more students demonstrating the behavior, post a few pieces of popcorn "in the bowl." When a predetermined number of popcorn pieces is earned, reward the class with a popcorn party.

Student Discipline Log

SUBJECT:			
M			
T	Call a difficult student after a good day.		
W			
T			
F			

		NOTES:
Recognize every student's special qualities.		

Back-On-Track Activities

When students enter the room full of energy (after lunch, recess, p.e. or an assembly), behavior problems often occur and teaching time is lost. Conduct quick, simple activities to focus students' attention on you as soon as they walk through the door:

- a game of Science and Health Hangman
- a Math Brain-Teaser
- a Social Studies Who-Done-It Mystery
- a game of 21 Questions
- stretching, breathing or relaxation exercises

By the time the activity is finished you will have assembled a captive audience for your next lesson.

SSR Siesta

Now that the weather is warming up, a good way to reward appropriate behavior is with an "SSR (sustained silent reading) Siesta." When the class earns a predetermined number of points, take them outside for a relaxing session of silent reading. Have each student bring a book, a small blanket or beach towel, and perhaps a throw pillow. Serve lemonade and cookies once students are settled and reading.

Student Discipline Log

_____
_____
_____
_____
_____
_____
_____
_____
_____
_____

NAME: WEEK BEGINNING:

SUBJECT:			
M			
T	Have students choose a goal to work towards.		
W			
T			
F			

		NOTES:
Keep your plan in effect until the last day.		

End-of-the-Year Recognitions

Make sure every student leaves your class with a feeling of pride. Prepare awards that spotlight students' special qualities. Here are a few ideas:

- The "Bright-Idea" Award (to a student who contributed original ideas to the group)

- The "Peace Prize" Award (to a student with a flair for mediating peer conflicts)

- The "I Can Do It" Award (to a student who didn't easily give up on a task)

- The "Picasso" Award (to a student who demonstrated artistic talent)

- The "MVP" Award (to a student who demonstrated exceptional athletic ability)

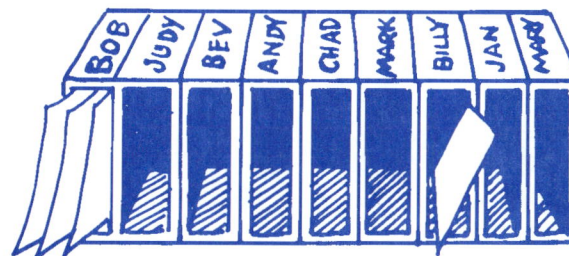

Mail Station

Before students part for summer vacation, give them an opportunity to exchange compliments, thank you's and happy-summer wishes. Plan time each day for students to write to one another. Set up a "mail station" for these special deliveries:

- Glue rectangular boxes side by side to form student "mail slots." Label the top of each box with a student's name.

- Have students deposit their "mail" into the appropriate slots. Encourage them to make sure every box gets plenty of mail.

- Select a student to be "postmaster" and deliver the mail to students on the last day of school. Allow volunteers to read their letters aloud.

Student Discipline Log

_____

_____

_____

_____

_____

_____

_____

_____

Positive Recognition Ideas

Positive reinforcement is the key to effective discipline. You can't change behavior just by using consequences. Consequences merely *stop* behavior. If you want to *change* behavior, you must use positives. The following ideas and those listed on each page in your Plan Book should help you to provide consistent positive reinforcement throughout the year.

Positively Speaking

Verbal reinforcers are the most accessible vehicle you have to demonstrate that students are behaving appropriately. Remember that all human beings need positives. Praise students daily!

Hand-in-hand with positive verbal responses go nonverbal responses. A smile, a wink, a pat on the shoulder or a positive gesture can clearly communicate your support for appropriate behavior. Use these responses often with all of your students.

Classroom Jobs

Many teachers simply rotate classroom jobs or "privileges." Instead of assigning these tasks routinely, have your students earn the right or privilege of doing the following:

- Leading the line
- Distributing lunch tickets
- Being team captain
- Passing out paper
- Giving out playground equipment
- Choosing a game
- Helping the teacher after school
- Leading the Pledge of Allegiance
- Designing the bulletin board
- Grading papers

Elementary students especially love to help out in the classroom. By having them earn the right to do so, it becomes even more special.

Marbles in a Jar

This technique enables all students to receive positive recognition. The sound of the marble reinforces the appropriate behavior each time you put a marble in the jar. Follow the guidelines below:

- Whenever *one* or *more* students behave, they earn a marble for the entire class.
- Each marble equals one point. When the class earns a predetermined number of points, they earn a reward (extra free time, for example).
- The students earn a large number of marbles each day or period.

  Elementary: one marble per student per day (for problem students increase number of marbles).

  Secondary: five marbles per period (for problem students, increase number of marbles).
- The class earns the reward quickly.

  K–3rd grade: one day

  4th–6th grade: one–five days

  Secondary: one week–two weeks
- The class always earns the reward on time.
- The reward must be something students want.
- Never take marbles out of the jar.
- At the end of each day or period count the marbles earned and keep a running total.
- Use peer pressure, for example: No rules broken—five-marble bonus
- Give direction, then reinforce with marbles.

At the secondary level, use a different jar for each class period. This creates competition between classes. This idea works well for special classes (music, art) at the elementary level.

Grab Bag

This is an excellent positive motivator for one child or for the entire class. The students can earn tickets to the Grab Bag by exhibiting appropriate behavior. Each "grabber" may take one card out of the Grab Bag. On the card is written the reward the student has earned. Here are some examples of awards teachers have used with their classes.

- Right to be monitor
- Right to be team captain
- Right to be first in line
- Right to be teacher's aide
- Positive note to parents
- Extra free item
- Special free-time activity
- Free time with teacher
- Choose next class story
- Choose p.e. game
- Take care of class pet
- Miss one homework assignment
- Candy bar
- Arts and crafts supplies

Free-Time Passes

These are additional great motivators to use with individual students or the entire class. The "passes" are given to the students in recognition of their positive behavior. The student's name and amount of time he or she has earned are written on the pass. It is helpful to have a list of Free-Time Activities the students can choose from. Some activities teachers have used include:

- Arts and crafts
- Puzzles
- Games
- Special projects
- Special books
- Extra computer time
- Tutoring younger students
- Science projects
- Play with toys from home
- Help the teacher
- Help the principal

The Right to Rent

All classrooms have numerous items that the student would enjoy taking home and "renting" overnight or for the weekend. When students engage in desired behavior they can earn "rental cards" that specify the item the student has the right to rent and for how long. It is an incentive to have a specific list of items the students know they can rent. Among the items teachers have utilized as rentals are:

- Reading books
- Magazines
- Games
- Puppets
- Art and crafts supplies
- Puzzles
- Research materials
- Pets
- Game books
- Records
- Science equipment
- Comic books
- Special projects

It may be necessary to check with or notify the students' parents before classroom items are rented.

Positive Peer Pressure

We are all aware of how classmates encourage and reinforce a problem student's disruptive behavior. This negative peer pressure is often a critical motivating factor of problem behavior.

This same peer pressure with a positive direction can prove an invaluable aid in motivating problem students to improve their behavior. This is how it works. Set up a contingency in the classroom for the entire class to earn the positive they want if a selected problem student (or students) improves his or her behavior.

> For every hour Mike does his work without talking back, he will earn the class one point. When the class has ten points, they will receive fifteen extra minutes of p.e.

For every period Brenda does her work without fighting or yelling, the class will earn one point. When Brenda has earned the class twelve points, that day's homework assignment will be canceled.

One can clearly see how such contingencies can create an atmosphere in which classmates will pressure the problem students to behave. This may be the first time such students have received positive peer pressure and it can have a dramatic effect.

A positive peer pressure contingency must include:

- The behavior(s) you want the problem students to engage in (work without talking back, for example)
- What reward or privilege the class will earn (extra p.e.)
- How the class will earn the reward (every hour student does work earns one point, and when ten points have been earned, the class receives a reward)

Positives for All Grade Levels

Here is a list of effective positive reinforcers that can be used with individual students or the entire class.

Elementary-Level Positives

For Individual Students:

- Smile-O-Grams or Happy Grams or other positive notes sent to parents
- Free time for good behavior
- Positive phone calls and progress reports
- Work as classroom helper
- Immediate rewards, treats, stars, stickers, stamps, etc.
- Lunch with teacher
- Citizen of the Day or Week
- Work with custodian or librarian
- Wear special button or badge
- Take home classroom pet
- Special chair
- Spotlight student's work
- Extra library or computer time
- Food—raisins, peanuts, etc.

For the entire class:

- Extra recess
- Popcorn party or other party
- Special principal visit
- Extra movies or cartoons
- Special lunch
- Cooking activity
- Extra free time
- Special arts and crafts project
- Field trips
- Public recognition of group by principal
- Group photographers
- Extra p.e. time
- Special class visitor (firemen, magician)

Middle/Secondary-Level Positives

For individual students:

- Positive note or a call to parents
- Free time in class
- One-day extension on homework assignment
- Gift certificate for food or other treats donated by local merchants

For the entire class:

- Free time in class
- Play radio (cassettes, CD's) in class
- Give certificates for food and other items donated by local merchants
- Extra p.e., special or free activity day on Friday
- Earn time to participate in schoolwide art or student council project
- Classroom party
- Earn invitation to special assembly or movie
- No homework

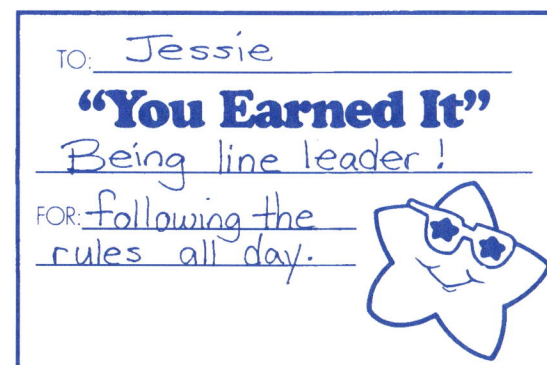

TO: _Jessie_

"You Earned It"

Being line leader!

FOR: _following the rules all day._

50 Opportunities to Say "You're Terrific"

There are hundreds of opportunities to praise students each day of the year. Don't let these moments slip by.

Praise students for:

1. entering the classroom quietly.

2. putting away coat and backpack.

3. cooperating while teacher takes attendance.

4. returning permission slips and school forms on time.

5. transitioning into an activity appropriately.

6. following directions.

7. saying "please" and "thank you."

8. listening attentively.

9. helping a classmate.

10. lining up.

11. turning in homework.

12. being a good audience at an assembly.

13. beginning work right away.

14. asking questions when unsure.

15. good behavior during a test.

16. participating in a class discussion.

17. walking appropriately in the halls.

18. working cooperatively with a partner.

19. good behavior during a field trip.

20. cleaning up.

21. good effort on an assignment.

22. assisting a new student.

23. sharing school experiences with parents.

24. making up missed assignments.

25. making a new friend.

26. good effort on a long-term project.

27. sharing.

28. being sensitive to others' feelings.

29. learning a new skill.

30. appropriate use of school property.

31. returning borrowed books and materials.

32. showing enthusiasm.

33. being responsible for a classroom job.

34. offering help without being asked.

35. not wasting paper and supplies.

36. staying on task.

37. telling the truth.

38. accepting a new challenge.

39. behaving when a guest is in the room.

40. reading at home.

41. participating in school functions.

42. demonstrating a positive attitude.

43. giving one's best effort.

44. returning from the yard quietly.

45. participating in a group activity.

46. using problem-solving skills.

47. showing creativity.

48. keeping busy when work is finished.

49. taking turns.

50. working cooperatively with a partner or group.

Strategies for Dealing with Difficult Students

If you follow your classroom discipline plan, consistently provide positive reinforcement for appropriate behavior, redirect students' nondisruptive off-task behavior and provide consequences for disruptive behavior, you will be successful in eliminating most of the behavior problems you face.

However, there will invariably be one or two students whose behavior is so disruptive to you and to the rest of the class that they require special attention.

Use the following strategies to deal successfully with difficult students.

Build Trust and Positive Relationships

Students who experience failure year after year often lack trust in their teachers and therefore are not willing to meet behavioral expectations at school. It is essential to reach out to these students to build their trust and develop positive relationships with them.

Plan the following activities:

Phone home or send a note before the school year begins.

Call the student's parents to assure them that you will do everything possible to make this a terrific year for their child. Let the parents know that you are looking forward to working together for their child's success.

Treat the student the way you would want your child to be treated.

Respond to the student in a caring, empathetic manner, just as you would want a teacher to respond to your own child.

Spend one-to-one time with the student.

Take a few minutes during class, at recess, during lunch or after school to talk with the student one to one about nonacademic issues. The student will enjoy having your undivided attention.

Call the student at home after a good day.

Make a quick phone call to offer some well-deserved words of praise. If the student isn't home, share the good news with parents and have them deliver the positive message later.

Call the student at home after a bad day.

End a difficult day on a positive note by phoning the student to get things back on track. Listen to what the student has to say. Express your confidence that tomorrow will be a better day.

Make get-well calls.

When a student is ill, pick up the phone and call to find out how the child is feeling. Both parents and student will appreciate your caring and concern.

Meet with Students for One-to-One Problem-Solving Conferences

A one-to-one problem-solving conference is a meeting between you and your student to discuss a specific behavior problem. The goal of this conference is not to punish but to listen to the student and give caring and firm guidance.

Follow these steps when conducting a one-to-one problem-solving conference:

1. Show empathy and concern.

Let the student know that you care about him or her, and that you are meeting to offer help and guidance, not to punish.

2. Question the student to find out why there is a problem.

Don't assume you know why the student is misbehaving. Ask questions.

"Did something happen today to get you so upset?"

"Are other students bothering you?"

"Do you have trouble seeing the board?"

"Is the work too difficult for you?"

"Is there something happening at home or in your neighborhood that's causing problems?"

3. Determine what you can do to help.

After listening to what the student has to say, you may discover a simple solution for correcting the problem (for example, moving a student's seat).

4. Determine how the student can improve his or her behavior.

Brainstorm with the student what he or she can choose to do differently in the future to handle the problem more effectively. Teach new behaviors if necessary.

5. Agree on a course of action.

Combine your evaluation with the student's and agree upon a plan of action that both of you can follow to improve the situation. Make it clear to the student that you are serious about not allowing misbehavior to continue.

Develop Individualized Behavior Plans

When a student is not responding to the positives and consequences in your classroom discipline plan, develop an individualized behavior plan to provide even more structured, more powerful interventions to help the student.

An individualized behavior plan includes:

- Specific appropriate behavior(s) required of the student.
- More motivating positive reinforcement.
- Stronger, more meaningful consequences.
- Relationship-building strategies.

Here is an example of an individualized behavior plan.

Individualized Behavior Plan

Appropriate Behavior:
– You will not talk without permission.
– You will stay in your seat.

Positive Support:
– For each 30 minutes that you do not talk out in class and you stay in your seat, you will receive a stamp on your chart.
– When your chart is filled, you will earn lunch with the teacher.

Corrective Action:
– If you continue to shout and get out of your seat and run around the classroom, you will be sent to another room for 15 minutes to calm down.

Relationship-Building Strategies:
Call at home after a good day.

Spend 5–10 minutes one-to-one time each day.

Enlist Support from Parents and Administrators

Gaining the support of parents and administrators is critical in solving problems with difficult students. Be proactive. Take the following steps to ensure you will obtain the support you need when problem behavior persists.

Deal with the problem on your own before asking for help.

Except in the case of severe misbehavior, you should attempt to handle a student's disruptive behavior on your own before you speak to the parents or administrator about the situation. Both will want to know what actions you have taken to help the student.

Document a student's behavior, and the steps you have taken to handle it.

When and if you do contact parents or an administrator about a problem, you will need accurate anecdotal documentation detailing the problem and the steps you have taken to deal with it. (Use the Behavior Documentation Record on page 103.) Documentation strengthens your position as a professional and communicates clearly that the problem does indeed exist.

Your anecdotal record should include the following information:

- Student's name
- Date, time and place of the incident
- A description of the problem
- Actions taken with the student

Keep these guidelines in mind when documenting problems:

- Be specific.

  Your statements should be based on factual, observable data. Avoid vague opinions.

- Be consistent.

  Document problems each time they occur. Repeated occurrences may show a pattern and be helpful in solving the problem.

Be sure to have your behavior documentation with you whenever discussing a student's problem behavior with parents or your administrator.

End-of-the-Year Checklist

Now that the year is closing, take a few minutes to assess how well you used Assertive Discipline to manage behavior in your class. Use the results to develop an even better program for next year.

Indicate: A=Always, S=Sometimes, R=Rarely

I Assumed an Assertive Attitude

☐ I felt in control of my classroom.

☐ I stayed calm whenever students misbehaved (I did not yell or become hostile).

I Developed a Classroom Discipline Plan

☐ The classroom discipline plan was posted in my classroom.

☐ The classroom discipline plan included rules, positive reinforcement, and a hierarchy of consequences.

☐ I followed the plan closely.

☐ I changed the plan when it wasn't working.

☐ I developed individualized behavior plans for chronically disruptive students.

☐ I informed the principal of the classroom discipline plan.

☐ I informed the parents of the classroom discipline plan.

☐ I provided a copy of the classroom discipline plan for substitute teachers.

I Taught the Classroom Discipline Plan

☐ I carefully explained the rules, positive reinforcement and disciplinary consequences to the students.

☐ I questioned the students to be sure they understood the plan.

☐ I reviewed the plan periodically to remind the students what was expected of them.

I Clearly Communicated the Rules and Specific Directions.

☐ I communicated my expectations to students at all times.

☐ My students knew what was expected of them at all times.

☐ I communicated to students in a clear, firm, and caring manner.

I Used Positive Recognition

☐ I positively recognized every student once a day.

☐ I used praise frequently.

☐ I used positives that students liked and looked forward to receiving.

☐ I changed the type of reinforcement I used when it wasn't effective in motivating students to behave.

☐ I changed the positive ideas periodically.

I Used Redirecting Techniques

☐ I consistently redirected students who strayed off task and were not disruptive.

I Provided Disciplinary Consequences

☐ I consistently provided consequences when students were disruptive or continually off task.

☐ I consistently followed through on the consequences promised.

☐ I provided consequences in a calm, assertive manner.

☐ I changed the consequences when they weren't effective.

If you find that you are weak in one particular area, review the new and revised *Assertive Discipline®* text and workbooks.

Ideas to Use Again

SEPTEMBER

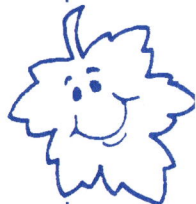

OCTOBER

NOVEMBER

DECEMBER

JANUARY

FEBRUARY

Ideas to Use Again

MARCH

JUNE

APRIL

JULY

MAY

AUGUST

Positive Parent Communication Log

List students' names. Each time you positively communicate with a parent, write the date in the box and indicate the type of contact with an "N" for note or "P" for phone.

Sample: 1/7 P or 3/5N

Names	Date/Type of Contact

Behavior Documentation Record

Make copies of this page to use throughout the year.

Student Name	Date/Time	Place	Problem Behavior	Disciplinary Action Taken

Student Roster

	Student Name	Address	Parent(s) Name(s)	Home Phone	Work Phone
1.					
2.					
3.					
4.					
5.					
6.					
7.					
8.					
9.					
10.					
11.					
12.					
13.					
14.					
15.					
16.					
17.					
18.					
19.					
20.					
21.					
22.					
23.					
24.					
25.					
26.					
27.					
28.					
29.					
30.					
31.					
32.					
33.					
34.					
35.					